PROPHETS
⌒◦◦❧ FOR ☙◦◦⌒
PRAYERS
PREYERS FOR PROFITS

Wayne Cade

ISBN 978-1-63903-106-1 (paperback)
ISBN 978-1-63903-107-8 (digital)

Christian Faith Publishing, Inc.
832 Park Avenue
Meadville, PA 16335
www.christianfaithpublishing.com

Printed in the United States of America

I am convinced after years of involvement with the institutional church that the advice and counsel I offer you through the following pages is patently clear and abidingly true. It does not require great analytical skills nor does it require powers of prophetic discernment to reach the regrettable but inevitable conclusion that these are difficult days for the church. The reality is that people are sick of the church, yet at the same time, they are truly hungry and thirsty for God. But the church has come upon hard times. If religion is to be relevant, it needs to address the point of your need. Weekly, a pastor comes with a sermon that is measured for effect; written with precision and spoken with articulate grace, and yet what good is it? What good is preaching if no one is saved, no one is delivered, if sin is never challenged, and wickedness never taken to task? While the Bible has been written some centuries ago, it has some prevailing principles intended to be applied to our current condition today.

Since the creation of man and up to our present age, man has been engaged on a journey to know and understand our Creator, which is known in the Christian community as seeking the kingdom of God. Man must make an unyielding decision and have a strong determination in order to unravel and follow the principles for seeking and serving the kingdom. After discovering God and after examining the deeds and details of his own life, man must then embark on the next phase of the journey. This phase consists of continuous spiritual growth, which is marked and measured as a process of spiritual maturation, from where man can then enjoy fellowship with God as well as experience the true worship of God.

Consequently, for many men this journey has led them to the doorstep of the church where many claimed to have arrived at the destination of their pursuit. However, despite popular notions to the contrary, conversion alone is not equivalent with spiritual maturity. Only devotion to the study of the scriptures on both personal and group levels. In addition to practicing, the principles revealed through those studies is real spiritual maturity acquired. While church attendance does afford one fellowship with others in the assembly, that alone will leave one stagnant in their spiritual development, and it's insufficient to be equated with or to advance one's spiritual maturity.

At the time of this writing, there are over 446,000 churches, synagogues, and mosques in the USA. Within these three religions, we find two common threads—the first is the Abrahamic thread, and the second would be the demonic thread. The latter of the two shall conduct my thought for the purpose of this book. While it is not my contention that either Judaism or Islam are exempt from the many problems that persist in the Christian community, I have no extensive knowledge of Judaism or Islam, so my conclusions are only referring to Christianity.

When man in pursuit of the kingdom of God arrives at the doorstep of the right church (he or she is spiritually viewed as a babe in Christ), he should be encountering a pastor who is able to lead him to salvation. One who, with the sensitivity of a shepherd's heart, is able to encourage new converts and to inspire them to godly living. For the job of all apostles, prophets, evangelists, and pastors is to share with both men and women the process of spiritual growth. This job, as the apostle Paul describes it, is for the purpose of "perfecting the saints for the work of the ministry and for edifying the body of Christ."

If a man or woman without any biblical literacy or familiarity with the spiritual developmental process unites with the wrong church, he places him or herself in a vulnerable position. The authenticity of their conversion experience is called into question, and the lives they lead will be contradictory to the faith they proclaim. Consequently, instead of being evangelized, they end up antagonized before realizing that it is possible to have ugly religion in what they thought was a beautiful church. They're also susceptible to unquestionably accept the Word from those misleading deceivers that I refer to as preyers in the pulpit (also biblically described as wolves in sheep's clothing) who attempt to amuse the masses with their own pretensions of power, influence, and popularity. The seekers will inadvertently capitulate to the whims of the supposed prophet (wolf) who's only there for profit. In doing so, they even subject themselves to potential financial and sexual abuse.

At this point on man's journey, he has already been converted and is now seeking an understanding of the will of God for his life. This goal of seeking the kingdom and the subsequent understanding of God's will carries with it no financial obligation nor any need for sexual exploitation. The primary reason for anyone to be involved with any church is because the church is supposed to represent a community of people who have the kingdom as their destination. The design of the gospel is to alter, to convict, to convert, to construct or reconstruct, to regenerate, and to bring one's solitary life into a wholesome relationship with God. If none of these things happen in the church with which you're united, then without a doubt, you're involved with a church that is lame, and one where there has been a failure to perform in relationship to the contractual promise of the gospel. Your mental, physical, emotional, financial, and personal prosperity is somehow caught up in this thing called the kingdom.

There are some who are engaged in this pursuit of the kingdom who wind up taking the wrong road, which will likely lead to what I call a "preyer for profit" pavilion. There, they wind up being, as the Scriptures say, "tossed to and fro, carried about by

every wind of doctrine, by the slight of men and cunning crafti-
ness, whereby they lie in wait to deceive."

Many have ventured into one of these "preyer for profit"
pavilions looking for inspiration, only to find insult. One claim-
ing membership there exposes himself to two of the most common abuses (financial and sexual) prevalent in these spiritual crack
houses disguised as churches. All of the "preyer for profit" pavilions
are little more than religious nurseries catering to spiritual midgets
and where the supposed worship is conducted only at the altar of
tradition. When one discovers himself united in such a place, they
then have a legitimate cause to change religious affiliations.

One cannot afford to be engaged in ecclesiastical games or
Sunday morning foolishness because it would be detrimental to
the spiritual fabric of their own lives. These pavilions, in an effort
to attract many, will attach a variety of Christian names on their
doors, but inside one discovers that the anchors of godly activity
are tied up by the bandages of apprehension and fear. The potential victims, when visiting these places, may initially experience a
level of excitement or comfort during the service or show, which
prompts them to return regularly to repeat or exceed their initial
experience. They unwittingly run the risk of becoming religious
thrill-seekers looking for whoever or whatever can fill their spiritual thirst for the moment. It is my belief that even in that sce-
nario the true spirit of the Living God attempts to communicate
through the spirit that the individual is in the wrong place. But the
individual is unable to discern the spirit's urging due to their own
spiritual immaturity and remains inadvertently in thrill-seeking
mode.

I want you to know that in these so-called churches, you
have pious pygmies and spiritual midgets who are looking only
for excitement at church, who need to be made aware that you
can do all the shouting and jumping up and down that you want
during the service and all that means is you'll be worn out when
you land in hell. As we enter the second fifth of this twenty-first
century, it appears that the demonic spirits are, at least, leading or

at best dominating these pavilions disguised as churches. While this phenomenon appears to be growing, it should be of concern as well as alarming to all avid adherents of Christianity. One can trace part of this thread of demonic influences in the church today as far back to the time of Jesus, when he had to run the money changers out of the temple area. Even in those days, while there was no known sexual exploitation, church leaders were corrupt and enriched themselves off the backs of those seeking God and true worship.

During those times, the priest would, by prayer, intercede on behalf of the parishioners because of the access that only the priests had. This presumed access back then is now available to all believers because Jesus has torn down the middle wall of partition. When the priests back then had sole access, this made the priest highly esteemed among the people. It also, in most instances, afforded the priest a lavish lifestyle compared to others in their communities, which likely stemmed from the misuse of the tithes and offerings received by the church. If one conducts an honest analysis of many of our churches today, the overwhelming conclusion would be that these same problems persist in today's churches; and in some cases, it's much worse. Some of these preyers buy luxury items such as multiple homes valued in the millions, multiple expensive cars. They target women and children for sexual exploitation, and some even have their own personal aircraft, all at the expense of their congregations. Many of them have perfected the craft on grooming some underage members for sexual exploitation. For anyone who doubts the existence of corrosion taking place in a lot of our churches today (if you allow me to pause parenthetically), I'll give one example.

Many church leaders today give support to our racist president, who lies to the American public daily; who obstructs justice; cages babies; prevents his criminal companions from going to jail; cozies up to dictators while shunning our allies; enriches himself, his family, and his friends; deliberately fails to participate in any congressional oversight efforts; and most likely cheats on his taxes. Despite the fact that the president lies and does all this other mess, a lot of churches have pastors who are supposed to represent truth, yet they faithfully and blindly support the president and also encourage their parishioners to do the same. I understand that God calls for us to pray for our leaders, but that doesn't mean we give our support and vote to them when their actions are clearly ungodly and some undoubtedly are criminal. That's why I'm inclined to believe that there is a point at which the church has a duty to speak or lose its right to be called a church. There's something fundamentally wrong with a religion that cannot or will not speak against the president's behavior. We need to question anyone who claims to be a man of God who, in spite of being aware of the policies and practices of this president, continues to unwaveringly support him.

There's been a misunderstanding of the relationship between the biblical priests and their congregants that has adversely influenced some of today's priests and pastors. Some decades ago, the craft of preaching was infiltrated by a brand of preachers who have no ability to be honest or prophetic as the position of preaching requires. Instead, they're only attracted by the perceived profit potential of the position. The appeal of the potential profits as a prophet has enticed many men and women to invest in studying at some theological school or seminary because in our times a personal calling to preach is no longer sufficient, nor is legitimacy as a pastor recognized unless one has a degree from one of those places. Remember, occasionally when Jesus had encounters with the Pharisees and Sadducees, they would contest his teachings primarily because none of them recognized him as a classmate in their own times of study. But academicians and teachers of the word may be astonished to learn that biblical knowledge and scriptural scholarship do not imply an advanced stage of spiritual development.

In other words, you can know all the Bible you want and still go to hell. What they all need to understand is that most of their degrees are just paper testimony to the elaborate cost of verified ignorance. Still today in order to be recognized and respected as a pastor, school is required, which supposedly certifies that you are a prophetic voice. When among your pastoral colleagues, the two most important things they want to know is where you went to school and the size of your congregation. These days what matters the most to a growing number of pastors is not the number of souls saved or lives changed but instead the focus is on the sizes of the congregation plus the tithes and offerings collected.

And due to the spiritual immaturity of some congregations, this breed of pastors is literally robbing their confused parishioners every week without a gun and without any threat of being arrested or being held accountable. As this is happening, you have a host of pastors who sit silently on the sidelines in the face of this abuse and in their own form of impotence they just say "Let us pray for them." God has not only given you a voice but a body also to go confront these fake prophets. The only manner by which religion becomes relevant is that someone comes to a point of discovery where silence is iniquitous, and a refusal to speak is irresponsible. Where would the church have been if those who had a duty to speak remained silent?

- Moses spoke to the pharaoh because in the face of injustice, something had to be said.
- Elijah spoke to Ahab and Jezebel because in the face of idolatry, something had to be said.
- Nathan spoke to David because in the face of adultery, something had to be said.
- Esther spoke to Artaxerxes because in the face of oppression, something had to be said.
- Ezekiel spoke to dry bones because in the face of death, something had to be said.
- Jesus spoke to Legion in a cemetery because in the face of a lost identity, something had to be said.

I do not intend to confuse my readers, so let me make it clear that I am not suggesting that all or even a majority of pastors and priests are preying on their congregations. But for the ones who are, we see their numbers are increasing only because of the silence of those around them. And all the priests and pastors who are not like-minded have a moral obligation to bring it to the light of exposure in order to help eradicate that mess. Any pastor who is aware of the abuse of the gospel by another pastor and fails to address it by any or all methods, including prayer, needs to take a self-examination to ensure that they themselves are not preyers for profits. No more sealed lips! There are some circles in which what-the church says is expected to be politically correct and socially acceptable. But in this age of cultural confusion and moral ambiguity, it is time for somebody to say something.

Sometimes, to speak in this environment is to live with personal discomfort, but to remain silent is to live with religious irresponsibility. There are moments when to speak is to ensure the rejection of secular society, but to remain silent is to ensure a disturbed conscience by day and a restless sleep at night. We must decide to either uphold our commitment to truthfully and passionately minister the gospel or choose to be complicit by silence to the misleading of seeking souls. Some ministers of the gospel should be reminded that the task of preaching is more than reading and attempting to discern the canon of Scripture. It requires that the one undertaking this task must not forget their own personal experience as they preach to their congregations. When one is preparing to preach, if it is to be authentic, the pastor must be able to articulate a combination of the Word blended with a little analysis of how that Word speaks to today's congregants. In other words, they must find a way to blend a combination of their spirit and experiences with the leading of the Holy Spirit.

For one to really understand how these profiteers disguised as prophets ascend to their lofty positions, we need to call to the stage the very parishioners who are being misled and victimized. As I mentioned in the beginning, man in his genuine pursuit of God can wind up being ensnared by false prophets. These false prophets easily recognize and identify the vulnerability of these newcomers, and they soon begin grooming them for abuse. Sometimes the victims can be introduced by their parents, other family members, or even friends to these pavilions for profit. When the introduction is made this way, it is likely that the parent, sibling, or friend is operating out of their own spiritual immaturity and their own lack of discernment. Parents can unintentionally provide the victim for the eventual abuse and in most instances, the trusting parent is likely a single woman who is only entrusting the preyer with the child because she wants a mentor in her child's life.

But the victim winds up with a lifetime wound that cannot be erased therapeutically but can undoubtedly be removed by God. And in cases where the woman has no children, she herself may be targeted by the preyer for extramarital purposes. She knows he's married but cannot resist temptation triggered by lustful desires when complimented by the preyer. This, combined with her perception of the esteemed position of the preyer, makes her highly susceptible to victimization. Eventually, any resulting affair will come to light because this likely is not the only extramarital affair that the preyer is having. And when the first lady of the church winds being treated for a STD or some other revelatory incident that occurs, transparency will soon follow.

Not long ago, the Catholic Church was embroiled in a widespread scandal where priests were molesting boys for decades. This abuse persisted so long because of the confused state of the victims as well as the silence of the hierarchy of the church after receiving reports of the alleged abuse. Curiosity may kill the cat, but complicity kills a lot more. When claims of abuse were made, the Catholic Church's response was to shuffle offending priests to other parishes in an attempt to silence the outcry. This futile effort to patronize the victims and to possibly sweep the matter under the rug obviously failed as multiple civil and criminal cases were filed.

The Catholic denomination was not the only one to be exposed. More recently, we've seen a host of other church leaders from what's known as the Bible Belt get caught up in a scandal. The Bible Belt is the southern area of the country that ranges from Virginia down to Florida and from there westward to Texas then up to the southern borders of Ohio and West Virginia. These supposed church leaders (some self-titled as pastors, bishops, apostles, prophets, and prophetess) have engaged in a variety of abuses in their own congregations. The major flaw found in each of these leaders is that they do not practice what they preach. Behind their deceptive, deceitful, fraudulent, underhanded, two-faced, treacherous dealings, they find ease manipulating members of their congregation who are spiritually less mature. And they're very selective of who to victimize because they do not want to be exposed.

Let me list a few of these preyers conduct in order to substantiate the validity of my argument. As previously noted, as early as 2002, the Catholic Church and their pedophilic charges resulted in both civil and criminal complaints. I will not list any names of the preyers involved out of my concern for any potential legal liability, but all of the following activity can be substantiated as it is a matter of public record for anyone interested specific details:

- St. Louis's pastor, without any religious study or degrees, was accused of misusing church funds to buy three vehicles (which included a Bentley) and a 2.8-million-dollar home, and he went to high-end stores on shopping sprees.
- In 2014, an Atlanta pastor solicits his megachurch members for help to pay for a sixty-five-million-dollar jet. He already has one. And in 2015, he was arrested for battery when his fifteen-year-old daughter said he choked and punched her at their home.
- A megachurch pastor in Houston, Texas, doesn't believe that Jesus is the only way to heaven, doesn't preach from the majority of the Bible, and uses very little scripture in

his sermons. He primarily preaches a prosperity gospel, which in essence reduces God to some cosmic bellhop to perform and provide for your needs.

- In 2018 in Richmond, Virginia, a sheriff's deputy, who was also a pastor serving as chaplain at a corrections facility where he worked, was charged with eight counts of sexual contact with male inmates. He eventually received four years in prison after being convicted of four of the eight counts.

- In 2010, at least four young men accused the pastor of a megachurch with over twenty-five thousand members in DeKalb County, Georgia, of using money, cars, and expensive gifts in exchange for sexual favors when they were teenagers. Eight years later, his married replacement pastor from a large church in Baltimore, Maryland, is accused of beating a female in New York in 2017. A month prior, he was in court for child support with a woman with whom he was having an affair which ended his marriage.

- In 2006, the president of the National Association of Evangelicals, who's married and had millions of followers, was found to have engaged in sex and drug use with a male prostitute over a three-year span.

- In 2007 Orlando, Florida, a pastor of a megachurch publicly admits to one of many adulterous affairs with strippers, which eventually ended in divorce. He was found dead last 2011 in a Manhattan, New York, hotel room with drugs on the scene.

- A popular TV show minister in Charlotte, North Carolina, from the 1970s to the 1980s, raped his church secretary, defrauded his flock, and was sentenced to forty-five years and served only five years.

- A 1980s televangelist admitted in 1988 to his involvement in a sex scandal with a prostitute.

- In 2013, for the first time in almost six hundred years, the Pope resigned from his position because of what's known as the Vatican leaks scandal, which involved the Pope and his personal secretary, and it revealed financial corruption, including bribery.

- In 2015 Spartanburg County, South Carolina, a pastor was arrested for having sex beginning in 2012 with a thirteen-year-old female, who was impregnated twice by the pastor and had two abortions.

- In 2017 Newport News, Virginia, a pastor diagnosed in 2015 with HIV was knowingly transmitting the disease to a man with whom he had a sexual relationship with in 2016.

- In 2018 Detroit, Michigan, a pastor was charged with murder in the death of a transgender woman. It was established during the trial that the pastor was a regular paying customer for sex with the transgender woman.

- In 2015 North Charleston, South Carolina, a pastor was accused of sexually abusing a minor female for years beginning in 2012.

- In Delaware County, Delaware, a pastor and his wife are charged with bilking one million dollars from 108 incapacitated seniors for whom they were supposed to be their guardians.

- On February 19, 2020, in Monroeville, Alabama, a married pastor was charged with two counts of sodomy, one with a person less than twelve years old and another a child victim who had to be hospitalized.

- In 2018 Portland, Oregon, police arrested a pastor, who lives in Georgia, on multiple sexual assaults including sodomy, rape, kidnapping, sexual assault, and identity theft. The cases involve three victims that began in 2012.

- In 2018 Charlotte, North Carolina, a pastor disappeared with nearly half a million dollars of investors' money. Returns without the money and vows to pay it back.

- In 2019 Charlotte, North Carolina, a televangelist known as the Maserati minister because of his expensive cars and one-million-dollar condo was convicted of tax evasion and sentenced to five years in prison.

- In 2016 Broward County, Florida, a pastor charged with molesting a thirteen-year-old dozens of times. The step-father of the thirteen-year-old was also accused of raping her.

- In 2016 Palm Beach County, a pastor was convicted of eleven counts of child sex abuse of three female victims, one as young as twelve years old. The abuse spanned over a three-year period, and the pastor's wife (also a pastor) was charged because she knew about the abuse but failed to report it.

- In 2017 Tallahassee, Florida, a husband caught his pastor having sex with his wife in his daughter's bed. The couple's son was reportedly sick at school and unable to reach the mother; the school called the father to retrieve the son. Upon arriving home with his son, the husband found them in his daughter's bed and threatened them both with a gun. However, the gun was not discharged.

- In Denver, Colorado, a pastor steps down after his wife exposes him for an adulterous affair with a church employee. The wife had struggled with her husband's infidelity for eight years.

- A Pennsylvania pastor, married with two adult children, was caught by the police in his car with a naked man bound with nylon rope in the front seat while he himself was in the back seat.

- In 2019 Charleston, South Carolina, a pastor was arrested for strangling a woman at the church who was eight weeks pregnant with his child. He's also the father of the woman's two other children. By the way, the pastor also is married.

- In 2019 Brooklyn Center, Minnesota, a pastor was convicted of drugging and sexually assaulting a woman at his church. Faces fifteen years in prison.

- In 2017 Toledo, Ohio, three pastors, one self-titled as prophet, were tried in an Ohio courtroom where one was convicted and two pleaded guilty to sex trafficking underage girls. One victim was fourteen when she moved into the first pastor's house, where she witnessed the pastor having oral sex with his stepdaughter, and he then enticed the stepdaughter and the new victim to have oral sex with each other while he recorded them. He then started having sex with the new victim for money multiple times a week over the next three years. He was convicted, and his wife was charged for trying to silence the victim. The pastor introduced her to the second self-titled apostle when she was fifteen. He began paying her for sex. He pleaded guilty. The teen eventually moved out of the pastor's house and met the third pastor, who also began paying her for sex. He has pleaded guilty, and his wife was charged for knowing about it but lying to the FBI.
- In 2018 Kansas City, Missouri, a pastor killed wife who was an associate pastor. The pastor was living a double life.
- In 2019 Sarasota, Florida, a pastor was arrested for sexual assault on a child under twelve years of age. The investigation into the pastor began in 2019 for abuses that dated far back as 1990. At least three people alleged that they were abused when they were boys by the pastor. There were two earlier investigations in 1990 and again in 2001–2002 that identified forty alleged victims, but the statute of limitations had elapsed on those cases.
- In 2015 Pennsylvania, a pastor molested fifteen kids, including his son, over a forty-year span within three different states.
- In 1998 Bristol, Tennessee, a preacher and wife convicted and sentenced to 179 years in prison for the charges of child abuse, kidnapping, and raping of their own daughter.

- In 2018 Prentiss, Mississippi, a married pastor was exposed during church service for having sex with her daughter for three years.
- In 2016–2018, Tipton County, Tennessee, after sexually assaulting two underaged boys in his home, a pastor faces forty-seven charges including rape, sexual battery, and enticing a child to buy alcohol. During the investigation, a third underaged victim was discovered.

These cases are just a snapshot of the activity going on with leaders in some of these "preyers for profit" pavilions. The question now is, How do we avoid joining one of these places? First, remember that one should never align oneself with a church simply because it's beautiful on the outside, because there are many beautiful churches, but the religion in some of them can be ugly. Whenever a church assumes the prerogatives of the past and fails to appropriate the priorities of the present, that's ugly.

Never join a church just because it's popular like one of the clubs you may attend on Saturday nights. This matter of how one selects a church or the basis upon which one selects a church is to be viewed in understanding that religion involves both attitudes and actions. It's not just a subjective experience, but it is also an objective activity. For anyone attending church and seeking to mature spiritually, group Bible study is more important than the one-way preaching from the pulpit. Bible studies afford you the ability to interact and ask questions within the group about how the scriptures relate to your condition.

Very often the churches to which some go to week after week are guilty of ignoring the pain predicament and failing to see the suffering in the lives of its own parishioners. More to the point, religion is ugly when it sees suffering and can't do anything about it. I did not say *won't*, I said *can't*; and if that's the case, then what you have is not just a religion that's ugly, but you also have a lame church that is incapable of altering the affairs of those with whom it comes into contact. Never join a church because the pastor is popular, may appear on TV, and seems to be godlier than anyone you've met.

There are many who make this mistake of viewing the preacher as a being holy as God while failing to realize the fact that the preacher is just as human as they are. It's common for new converts to esteem these pastors far above their worthiness because of their own spiritual immaturity. When one finds themselves united with the wrong church, this pattern of inappropriately esteeming the pastor will persist. But in the right church, along with gradual spiritual development by which the Christian life is marked and measured, the individual will soon view the pastor in the right light and appropriately give reverence to only God. It's the actions and the engagement of the church in the community that best determines it's beauty.

About the Author

He is a native Washingtonian, born and raised in District of Columbia. He joined a DC Baptist church (Metropolitan) in 1987. There he became active in the prison ministry and conducted a combination of weekly Bible studies and church services at the DC jail until 2004. He relocated from DC to Gaithersburg, Maryland, in 1994. He eventually became involved with the United Methodist Church. And in 2008, he discontinued his DC jail ministry and became active in the Montgomery County Detention Center's volunteer services where he remains active at the Hagerstown Department of Corrections in a men's study group, and he conducts monthly church services with a team of volunteers.

He is a retiree from Montgomery Department of Transportation.